The Battle Book
Warfare
by
Duct Tape

After reading about ancient world history, we became very fascinated by ancient weapons and warfare. We decided to make our own shields, swords and other weapons so that we could act out the history that we had learned.

We had so much fun fighting wars and sieging fortresses with crushing defeats and historic victories with our friends, we wanted to write down the instructions and patterns so that other kids could battle and act out history, too.

Enjoy!

ISBN-13:978-1-942006-05-3

Table of Contents

"Had I sons I should train them as your husband intends to train your son. It may be that he will never be called upon to draw a sword, but the time he has spent in acquiring its use will not be wasted. These exercises give firmness and suppleness to the figure, quickness to the eye, and briskness of decision to the mind. A man who knows that he can at need defend his life if attacked, whether against soldiers in the field or robbers in the street, has a sense of power and self-reliance that a man untrained in the use of the strength God has given him can never feel. I was instructed in arms when a boy, and I am none the worse for it."

- G. A. Henty
St. Bartholomew's Eve

✠ Description of the Game

Battling is at least two teams fighting each other using weapons. We suggest using our foam weapons to minimize injuries.

Divide your players into two teams of about the same strength and even numbers. Say there are four big guys and four little guys. There should be two big guys and two little guys on each team.

Weather is no deterrent to battling. We have had battles in rain and heat.

Object of the game: divide and conquer your enemy!

More than one battle can be played. It is important to keep score of who wins each battle. The one who wins the most battles is the victor!

You can use fortifications. Tree houses work well. Piles of logs or even swing sets can be used.

Naval battles can be fought using non-motor boats such as canoes and row boats. To fight a naval battle, simply row up to them and fight them. Do not use throwing axes, they are not waterproof.

Hints~

If you use strategy, you are more likely to succeed. Strategy is taking advantage of natural objects; say a creek, a hill, thick bushes or deep woods. If the sun is at your back it will be hard for the enemy to see and you will have an advantage. If you and your men encamp upon a hill, you will have an uphill advantage. The advantage to being uphill is that you can charge down on the enemy considering it is easier to run downhill than up. You can also stay on the hill. It is easier fighting above your enemies than below them. If you have a creek, you and your men can go on the opposite side and use it like a natural moat. This will make it very hard to effect a passage. If there are thick bushes that are hard to get through, you can either hide in them and ambush your foes, or you can place your men so it is on one side of your army so they cannot outflank you. If you want to know more about strategy, read old books!

With fortifications, it is often wise to use your spear instead of your axe or sword. The spear has greater length which is helpful in forts. It is very wise to use missiles (water balloons, throwing axes, etc.) so you can bombard the enemy without having to storm the gate.

It is crucial to use shields. People who do not use shields are usually slain early in the battle and are vulnerable to throwing axes and heavy weapons such as battle axes.

Terrible war cries intimidate the enemy.

It is important to have one main leader (general). This keeps the army unified and reduces squabbles.

✠ Rules of the Game

Rule #1
Chivalry and honor must be exhibited at all times.

Rule #2
If any weapon hits your limb (for ex. arm, leg, hand), you are no longer able to use it.
If you are holding a weapon in the hand or arm that is hit, you can't keep using the weapon with **that** arm but could switch it to the other arm and keep fighting. If both arms are hit, you must surrender or run away.
If your leg is hit, you must limp. If both legs are hit, you must kneel or squat.
If you lose all your limbs, you are doomed!

Rule #3
If you get hit in the head, neck or torso, you are officially dead and can't play until the end of the battle.

Rule #4
The only way to win a battle is when all of the enemy (other team) is killed, has surrendered or has run away (escaped).
If a team holding prisoners is defeated, the prisoners are automatically freed.

Rule #5
If someone surrenders, you can either keep them captive, (they are not allowed to escape) or release them and they are free to return to their army (team).

Rule #6
Parley~ A parley is when one or possibly two people from each team talk to each other. To start a parley, one team member must say, "I request an audience." If the other team agrees, they send a person forward to talk to the other.
It is usually used for discussing the release of prisoners by ransom or switching of players. You can be chivalrous and release prisoners. It is important to not carry weapons but must leave them behind during a parley to avoid treachery.

Rule #7
We believe that only boys should battle with other boys. Young men should practice protecting young ladies so it is not appropriate to fight them.

Rule #8
Ransom~A ransom is when a soldier who is captured is released by a payment of money. You can make your own money by folding tin foil into circles, the shape of coins. To ransom a prisoner, first call a parley and then negotiate the price. A general usually costs more than the average soldier. (This rule is optional.)

Weapon Instructions

PVC pipe tips: You can find PVC pipe at your local hardware store like Lowe's and Home Depot. You will need a pipe cutter or a saw to cut the PVC pipe to the correct length. If you do not have a saw, the large hardware stores will usually cut it for you.

PVC pipe insulation~the black foam stuff. We usually buy this at the same stores as the PVC pipe. We like the kind that comes in a 4 pack of 3 foot pieces. It says on the package that it is for copper pipe but it works just fine for these weapons.

Foam~the 2 inch thick green stuff. You can find this foam at Wal-Mart and fabric stores like JoAnn.com and Hobby Lobby. It comes in small packages or in large pieces by the yard.

Cardboard: It can be difficult to cut cardboard so younger kids might need some help or supervision. In most of the pieces that use cardboard, it is important to cut the cardboard so the "ridges" (inner corrugated sections) **run across** the narrow width of the piece. This way the piece can bend properly. Check instructions before tracing the pattern onto the cardboard.

½ Width Piece of Duct Tape: Before we begin the weapon instructions, we need to define a term we will use in the book: "½ width". To make a ½ width piece of duct tape, take a piece of duct tape and tear it lengthwise (the long way). Now you have two ½ width pieces of duct tape. Sometimes, even a ¼ width piece of duct tape is used. Just tear the ½ width piece again to make the ¼ width.

Now, on to the fun!

Sword~

Materials:
3 foot piece of ¾ inch PVC pipe
3 foot piece of PVC pipe insulation
(We use 3/8" thick polyethylene foam, fits ¾" pipe)
Duct tape
Scissors
(You may need a saw to cut the PVC to size)
      Please Note: This project may require adult help to use the sharp tools.

Directions:
Cut 8 inches off of your 3 foot piece of insulation.

Next, take the larger piece of insulation and slide it down the 3-foot PVC pipe.

Leave about 1 inch extending off of the PVC at the point of the sword.

Take the 8 inch piece of insulation foam.
There is a seam down the length of it. Cut a slit 2 inches long on the seam in the middle (center) of the piece.
On the opposite side from the seam cut another slit.

Slide the piece of foam onto the PVC pipe to form the hilt of the sword.

Crisscross the duct tape around the hilt to strengthen it.

Tape across the end of the hilt, turn and do it again. Then tape around the end to make it smooth.
Do this on both ends of the hilt.

Cover the entire hilt with duct tape.
Be sure to wrap around the pipe/ handle.

Tape the point (end) of the sword blade the same way. Wrap the duct tape around a few times to strengthen it so it won't tear during battle.

Now tape the blade. It is helpful to have another person. Start at the hilt and wrap on a slightly diagonal angle towards the tip of the blade.

Cover the handle. Cap the end just as you did with the end of the blade.

Decorate as desired. Often wealthy Greeks and Romans would put a jewel in the center of the hilt.

Spear~

Materials:
4 foot piece of ¾ inch PVC pipe
1 foot piece of PVC pipe insulation
(We use 3/8" thick polyethylene foam, fits
¾" pipe)
Duct tape
Scissors
(You may need a saw to cut the PVC to size)

Please Note: This project may require adult help to use the sharp tools.

Directions:
Slide the 1 foot piece of pipe
insulation onto the PVC pipe.
Leave at least 2 inches extending
past the end of the PVC pipe.

Tape across the end of the
insulation at the tip of the spear,
turn and repeat. Then tape around
the end to make it smooth.

Starting at the tip, wrap the duct
tape on a slightly diagonal angle
until the insulation is covered and
just onto the PVC pipe.

Tape around the base of the blade over the PVC pipe to reinforce it.

Then, taking the color of your choice, tape a long strip down the length of the pipe. Smooth edges of tape.

Tuck end of the tape into the open end of the PVC pipe.

Repeat on the reverse side of the PVC pipe so that the handle is covered. It usually takes 2 strips of duct tape to cover the handle of the spear.

Decorate as desired.

Battle Axe~

Materials:

1 piece of foam 9" by 11" by 2" thick
3 foot piece of ¾ inch PVC pipe
Cardboard 4" x 12"
Duct tape
Scissors
Marker
Pattern
Saw (You may need a saw to cut the PVC to size)
      Please Note: This project may require adult help to use the sharp tools.

Directions:

Print and cut out the pattern. Lay the pattern on the foam, trace the blade of the battle axe
on the foam using a permanent marker and then cut it out.

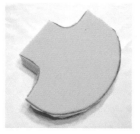

Bend the piece of cardboard in half. Place the blade next to the PVC pipe about 1" down
from the end. Fold cardboard over both of them and tape down the cardboard very well.
Make sure to go all the way around the base of the blade.

Tape diagonally to keep the pipe from sliding.

 Tape over the place where it crosses the PVC pipe.

Cover the tip of PVC pipe with duct tape.
Cover cardboard with duct tape.

 Use a long piece of duct tape to tape over the edge of the blade.

Wrap duct tape around to hold down the ends of that long piece.

Cover the blade with duct tape piecing diagonally in a fan shape from the cardboard around the edge to the other side and up to the cardboard.

Cover handle with duct tape.

Decorate to your liking.

Throwing Axe~

Materials:
1 piece of foam 5 ½" by 11" by 2" thick
Duct tape
Scissors
Marker
Pattern

Directions:
Print and cut out the pattern. Lay the pattern on the foam, trace the throwing axe on the foam using a permanent marker and then cut it out.

Cover the handle with duct tape the color of your choice.

Carefully tape the end so that the corners stay square.

  It is important to put a piece of duct tape on the side of the axe as shown in the picture to reinforce the axe. This prevents the throwing axe from tearing when you throw it.

Do this on both sides.

Press duct tape firmly to foam

Pinch the edges so they don't get dirty.

 Cover the inside of the blade.

Starting on the sides, cover the blade, being careful to keep the edges square.

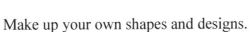

 Using the same technique, you can make throwing knives.

Make up your own shapes and designs.

DO NOT USE IN WATER!! They might get moldy. They are not waterproof.

Shield~

Materials:

Plywood, size and shape of your choice
Four (4) small blocks of wood 3 ½" x 1 ½" x ½"
Cardboard
Duct Tape
Four (4) Screws 1 ½" long (or long enough to go through the blocks of wood, cardboard and plywood)
Saw (to cut plywood if needed)
Screwdriver
Sandpaper
Scissors

     Please Note: This project may require adult help to use the sharp tools.

Directions:

Before you begin cutting the wood, plan how big you want your shield to be. We recommend you measure your arm from the elbow to the knuckles on your hand when you make a fist. The shield should be at least this wide.

Take a piece of plywood and cut to the shape (square, circle, oval, or rectangle) you want for the shield. Either sand the wood or cover the front with duct tape. You may want to add details with duct tape. Usually, we cover the front of the shield with duct tape and sand the back well so that we don't get splinters.

Cut a strip of cardboard 18" long by 4" wide. Cover with duct tape so as to strengthen it. Cut another strip of cardboard 12" long by 2" wide. Also cover with duct tape.

Bend up 1 inch on the ends and curve the rest of the piece of cardboard. Do this to both pieces.

Measure where the large piece of cardboard should go using your arm. Place it near your elbow. (You may need a friend to help you with this.)

Tape down the ends.

Place a block of wood on the end and screw down on each end of the block. Do this on both ends of the piece.
If you have a power screw driver you may want to pre-drill the holes. You can use a regular screwdriver also.

Measure where the smaller piece should go by placing your arm in the large piece. You will grip the smaller piece so place accordingly.

Tape ends to hold in place. Place a block of wood on the end and screw down on each end of the block. Do this on both ends of the piece.

It should look something like this when it is finished.

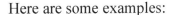

The shield is done. Decorate as you desire.

Here are some examples:

⊕ Ideas for Shields

Round or Circle Shield~
This shield was used by the early Germans, Greeks, Celts, Iberians, Goths, Etruscans, and other peoples. This type of shield was popular around the early 5th century. One of the earliest types of shields, the standard size was about 2 feet in diameter but it could be different sizes depending on the cultures. The Greek Hoplite shields were usually about 3 feet in diameter. Made of wood, usually painted in interesting designs, it had an iron or bronze boss in the center.

Rectangular Shield~
This shield was often used by Romans, Samnites and sometimes the Celts. Medes and Persians also used a rectangular shield. The earliest use of this shield was 200-300 B.C. by the Samnites.
The Roman shields were about 4 feet long by 2 ½ feet wide and were very effective. Made of wood, painted with the Roman thunderbolt design, it often had the legions symbol on it with an iron boss in the center.

Oval Shield~
The oval shield was used by the Carthaginians, Iberians, and the late Roman Empire. The Carthaginians used this shield around the 3rd century B.C. They averaged about 30 inches long by 25 inches wide. This shield was also made of wood with an iron or bronze boss which was often spiked. It could have been painted or unpainted, possibly with the Carthaginians' crescent moon symbol.

Norman Shield~

The Normans used to use round shields but when they started using horses more often they lengthened the bottom of the shield to give more protection to the leg. The Norman shield was approximately 5 feet long and 2-3 feet at its widest point. In 1,066 A.D., the Normans used this shield in the conquest of England against the Saxons. Painted with artistic designs, it was made of wood with a metal boss.

Medieval Shield~

Smaller than the Norman shield, this particular shield was a favorite to the armies of Christendom during the 12th-13th centuries. The top of the shield is straight and curves down to a point at the bottom resembling a triangle. It was about 3 feet long by 2 feet wide. Painted with the knight's coat of arms, this shield was wooden and had no metal boss.

✠ Helmet Instructions

Barbarian Helmet~

Materials:
Patterns
Cardstock
Cardboard
Duct Tape
Scissors
Clear "scotch" tape
Elastic~about ¾" wide by about 8 inches long (If you choose this option, see instructions)
Stapler/Staples

Directions:

Before we begin, we need to explain that there are two ways to make the back of the helmets. The first way will be shown with the Barbarian helmet and the other will be shown with the Greek helmet. Either way will work with both helmets.

Print the helmet pieces on cardstock and cut them out. (If you want the helmet in a smaller size, try minimizing the patterns on a copy machine.) Tape together the upper helmet pieces at the center front with the "scotch" tape.

Tape together the other edges at the top of the helmet pieces.

Cut a piece of cardboard 7" x 1 ½". Bend into a curve. Put a 9" piece of duct tape on it with 1" extending from each end.

Place on the front of the helmet right above the eye holes.

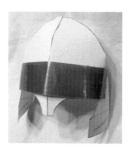

Tape over the band and around and through the eye holes.

Cut a piece of cardboard 3 ¼" x 1 ½". Tear a piece of duct tape about 5' long in half lengthwise. Put one piece of that tape on the cardboard (with tape extending past the ends of the cardboard) and tape it to the nose guard. Press the tape under the tip of the nose guard.

Tape on either side of the eye hole.

Cover the helmet upper with duct tape.

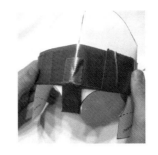

Tape lower helmet pieces to the upper helmet pieces, making sure they are even.

Cut two (2) pieces of cardboard 5" x 3". Taking a longer piece of duct tape, tape the cardboard to the sides. Line up next to the eye holes. Tape on the inside as well.

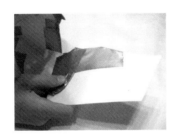

Optional: You can trim the edge of the lower helmet to line up smoothly with the upper, but it is not necessary.

Carefully tape around the eye hole, covering the cardboard. This is what you have now.

Cover the sides with duct tape.

To tape the bottom of the lower helmet together, first try it on to see how it fits. If you need to overlap the edges you can or you can just have them meet. Tape. If necessary, trim the edges. Cover with duct tape.

Cover the inside with duct tape. This helps the helmet last longer.

Cut a piece of cardboard 6" x 2 ½" and bend it into a curve. Attach to the lower helmet with tape. Cover with tape.

This is what you have so far.

For the back of the helmet: Cut two (2) separate pieces of cardboard the size of the back of the helmet piece. Bend into a curve. Tape onto back helmet piece.

Tape the back helmet piece to the top of the helmet. You can pinch the duct tape in the front and then trim it off. Tape the back helmet piece firmly on the sides of the top as well. Cover back helmet piece with duct tape.

Cut the elastic in half so that you have two (2) pieces about 4 inches long. Staple the pieces to the back helmet piece. Be sure to staple so the "pointy" part of the staple is facing outward.

Then try on the helmet. Adjust the elastic to fit and staple it to the helmet.

The Spike: This is optional but it makes the helmet look really awesome. Fold the spike pattern pieces on the dotted lines. Tape. Bend the tabs outward. Place on the helmet in the front and tape down. Cover with duct tape.

Decorate with colors as you desire.

You're done! Great job!

Greek Helmet~

Materials:
Patterns
Cardstock
Cardboard
Duct Tape
Scissors
Clear "scotch" tape

Directions:

Before we begin, we need to explain that there are two ways to make the back of the helmets. The first way will be shown with the Barbarian helmet and the other will be shown with the Greek helmet. Either way will work with both helmets.

Print the helmet pieces on cardstock and cut them out. (If you want the helmet in a smaller size, try minimizing the patterns on a copy machine.) Tape together the upper helmet pieces at the center front with the "scotch" tape.

Tape together the other edges at the top of the helmet pieces.

Tape lower pieces to upper pieces matching the overlap dotted lines.

Cut a small piece of cardboard (about 1" x 3") for the nose piece. Cover it in duct tape.

Try on helmet, center the nose piece and then tape it on to the center front.

To strengthen the sides, cut cardboard to fit and tape in place.

Cover entire helmet in duct tape.

To make the back of the helmet: Cut the back helmet piece out of cardboard and cover it in duct tape. Cut a piece of cardboard long enough to go all the way across the back of your head and 2 inches wide. Tape it to the crosspiece at the bottom of the back helmet piece. Cover it in duct tape. Tape the top of the piece to the top of the helmet.

Try on the helmet then tape the ends to the sides to make a firm back to the helmet as shown in the picture. (This is the first option for the back of the helmet. See the Roman helmet for the other option.)

This is what you have so far.

To make the crest: Cut 1 crest piece from cardboard. Cut 2 small rectangles about 1" x 3". Bend them in half to form an L (90° angle). Tape to the back of the helmet just a little past the top so they are standing up.

Put the crest piece between the small cardboard pieces and tape. The crest can be touching the helmet or be just above it.

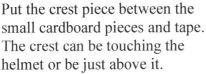

Cover the crest with duct tape. Use a different color if you prefer.

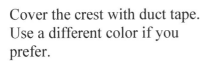

Attach front point of the crest to the front of the helmet.
We recommend that the inside of the helmet be covered in duct tape also. It helps it last longer.

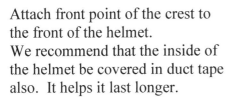

✳Costumes

Tunic~

Materials:
Some sort of fabric-knit, sheets, curtains, or whatever you have
Belt or material for a sash
Scissors
Sewing machine or needle and thread

Directions:
First determine the size you will need. Most tunics in the Greek and Roman time went down to the knees and had no sleeves. They draped over the shoulders a little bit. The size of your fabric may determine the width or measure across the shoulders. Make it wide enough so that you can slip it over your head and shoulders and get the arms out of the arm holes. If you have enough fabric, double the length so you won't need to sew a seam across the shoulders.

Cut a hole for the head to go through. The No-Sew Option is to just pull the tunic over the head and use a belt to keep it around the waist.

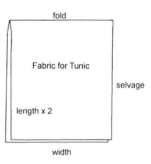

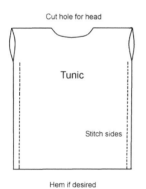

The sewing option is to sew up the sides but leave an arm hole. Hem the bottom if desired. Knit fabric is nice because it doesn't fray and you won't have to hem the edges.

In the early Roman times, soldiers only wore sleeveless tunics. It was considered too feminine to have sleeves. But near the end of the Roman era, it was acceptable to wear sleeves.

If you want sleeves in your tunic, make a "T" shape of fabric and then sew up the sides. Be sure the main body of the tunic is wide enough so that you can get it on and get the arms through the sleeves. Maybe almost double the width across the front of the person.

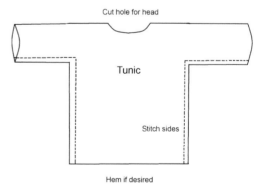

Some children are small and the hole in the neck will gap too much. Just add a button and loop at the back of the neck to close it a little. See Cloak instructions.

Use a belt or cut a strip of fabric to wrap around the waist. The tunic was considered underclothing that was worn under armor or a toga.

Cloak~

Materials:
Some sort of fabric-knit, sheets, curtains, or whatever you have
Button
Thin piece of elastic, ribbon, or string
Couple of pins
Scissors
Needle and thread

Directions:

Determine the size of cape that you need. Do you want a cloak that goes down to the knees or almost to the floor? That is your length measurement plus an inch to turn over at the neck. The width of your fabric may determine your width of the cloak, otherwise decide how wide you want it.

Cut your fabric to size. If you are using a fabric that will fray, you may want to hem the sides first. Fold over an inch the top edge which will go by the neck. Try it on. Clasp the cape closed a few inches down from the front of the neck. This where you will attach the button and elastic (ribbon). Mark it on both sides with a pin. Sew on the button on one side. Measure a small piece of elastic (ribbon) around the button so you can still get it on and off. Stitch elastic (ribbon) on both ends to the cape at the mark.

Throw over the shoulders and button at the neck.

The Romans wore pants under their tunics in cooler weather, so if you wear pants under your tunic you will still be authentic.

Money Pouch~

Materials:
Fabric: see instructions
String, rope, ribbon, shoe lace or whatever you have
Safety pin
Scissors
Sewing machine or needle and thread
Option: Leg from a pair of cut off pants

Directions:

You can make a money pouch out of almost anything. If you want a money pouch that is a bit fancier, you can use fabric. We just happened to have a scrap of velour that we used for a pouch. Knit fabric won't fray and is easier but any durable fabric will work.

Determine the size of pouch that you want. For example, if you want a pouch that is 5" x 7", allowing for seam allowances and the casing for the drawstring, cut two (2) squares of 6" x 8 ½". You can also cut a long rectangle and just fold over so that you eliminate one seam. The rectangle would be 6" x 16".

Put the right sides together and sew up the seams leaving one 6" side open (use ½" seam). Turn over 1" at the opening. Stitch around using a small seam of about ¼". On the side or center front, make a small cut in

the casing only on the front piece big enough for the drawstring to go through.

Cut your drawstring to at least twice the length of your opening. In this example, the opening is 10" after sewing, so the drawstring should be 20" long. Put the safety pin in the end of the drawstring and push it through the casing.

A leg from a pair of pants that was cut off into shorts can be made into a pouch. Cut to the size you want. Sew one end. Cut small slits about an inch apart and weave your drawstring in and out through the slits. If you don't have any, thrift stores and yard sales often have pants for cheap.

Coin Money for Ransom~

Materials:
Aluminum foil
Something heavy like a hammer or shoe

Directions:
Take a small piece of aluminum foil about twice the size you want the coin to be and fold in the edges to make a circle. It's all right if it is not perfectly round, ancient money wasn't perfect either. Press down firmly against a hard surface and then hammer flat with the heel of a shoe or a hammer.

Mark the coins with designs or figures so you know which coins belong to you. You can also make a money pouch to keep your money in while you are battling. See instructions for money pouch.

Battle Axe Blade

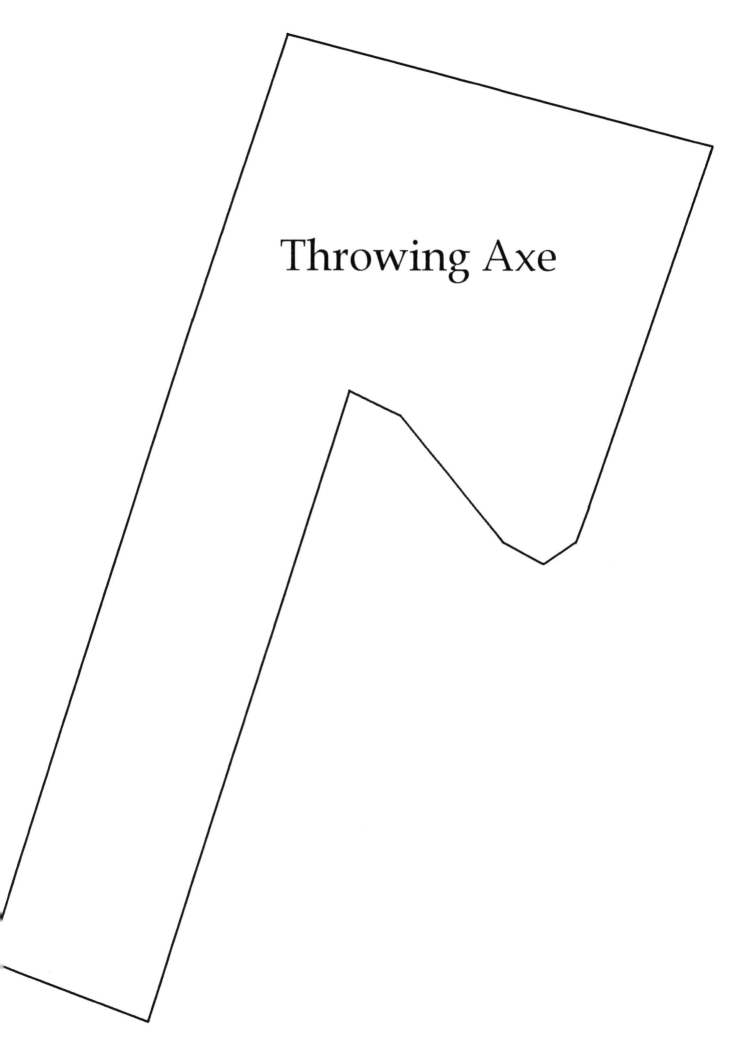

Throwing Axe

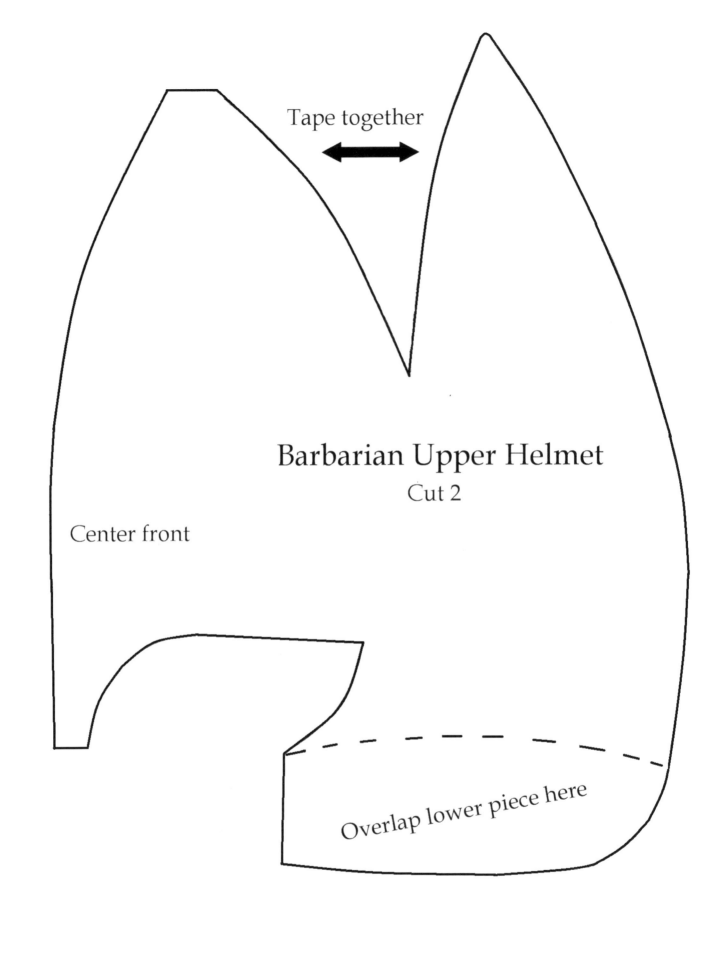

Tape together

Barbarian Upper Helmet
Cut 2

Center front

Overlap lower piece here

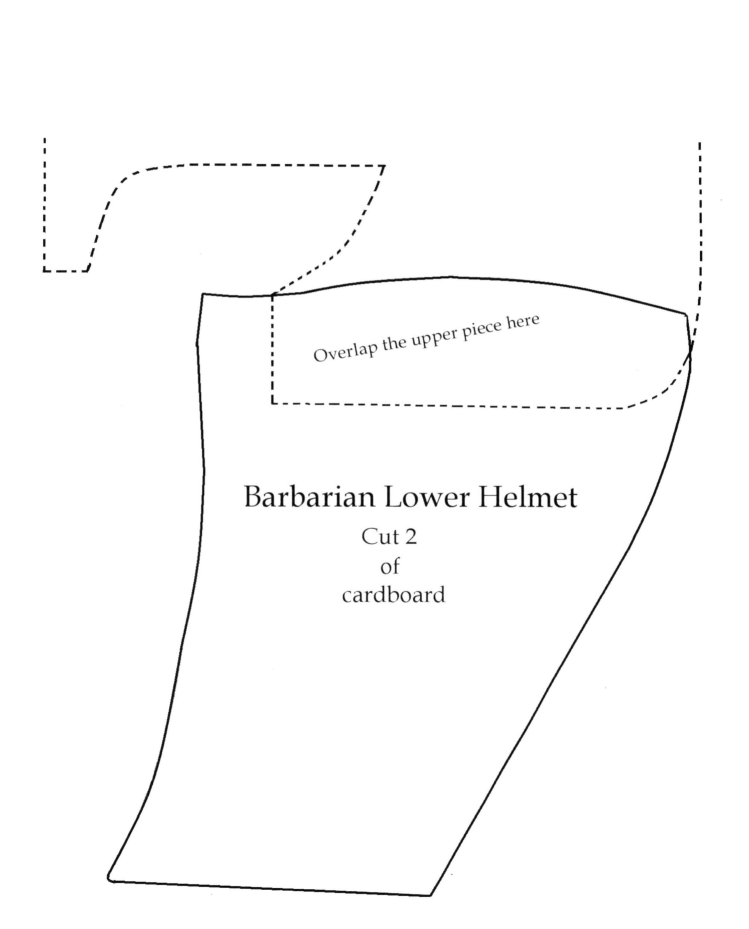

Overlap the upper piece here

Barbarian Lower Helmet

Cut 2
of
cardboard

Barbarian Helmet Spike

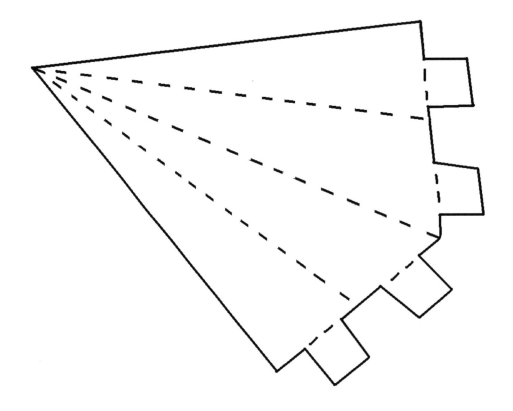

Cut 1

Fold on dotted lines

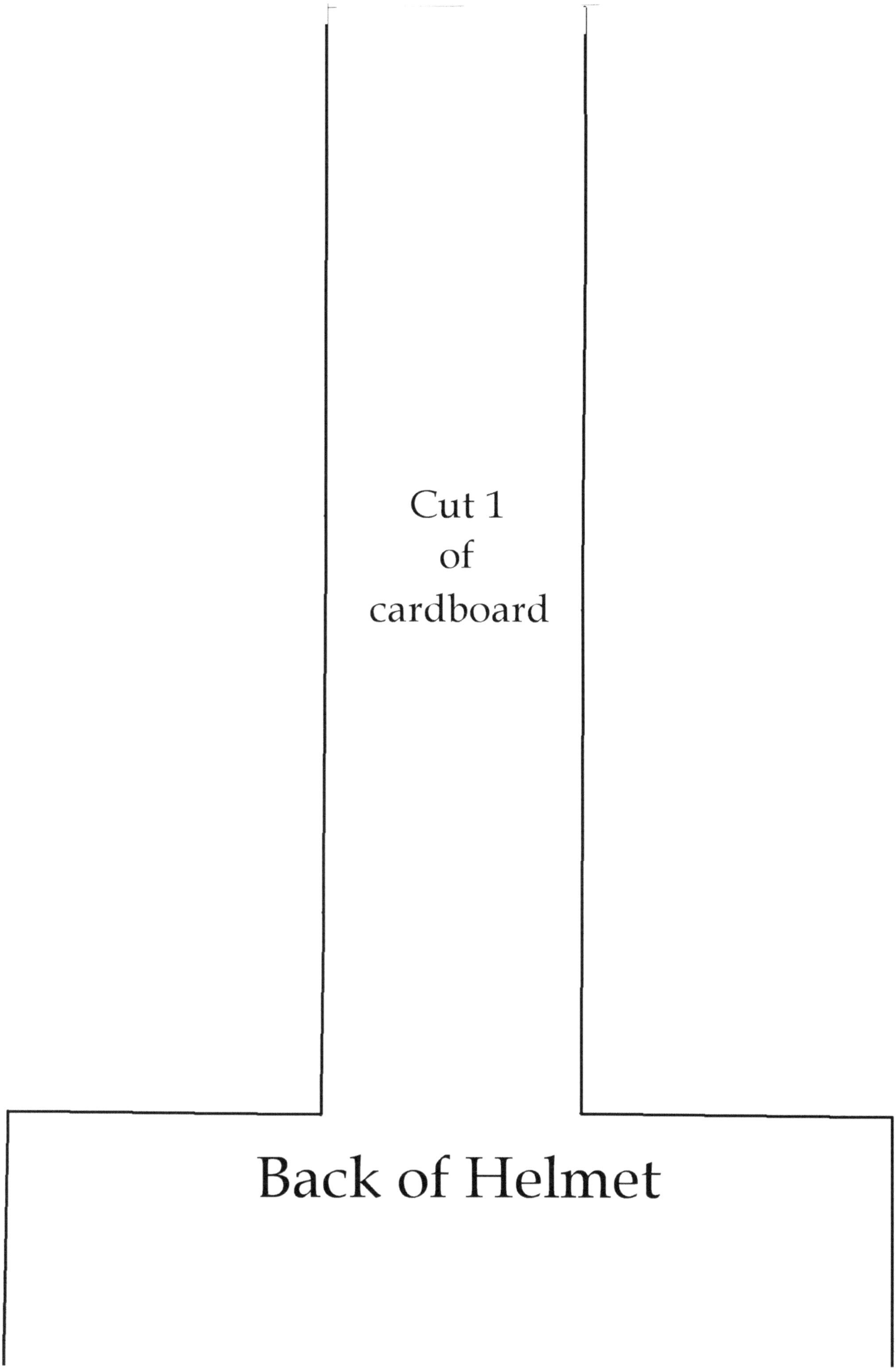

Cut 1
of
cardboard

Back of Helmet

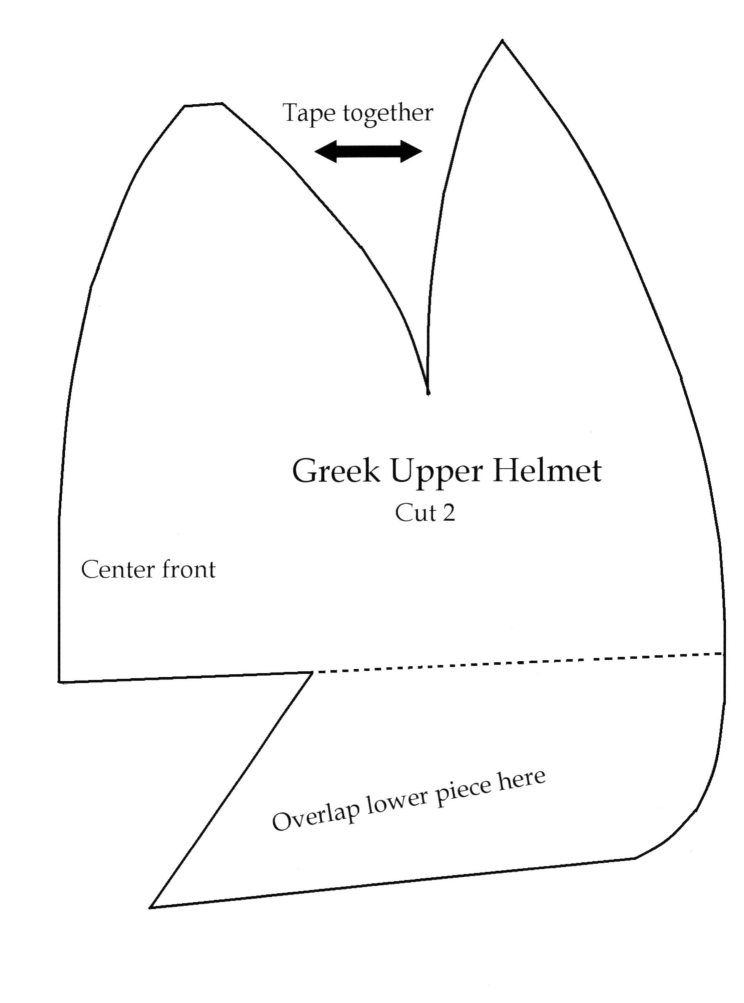

Tape together

Greek Upper Helmet

Cut 2

Center front

Overlap lower piece here

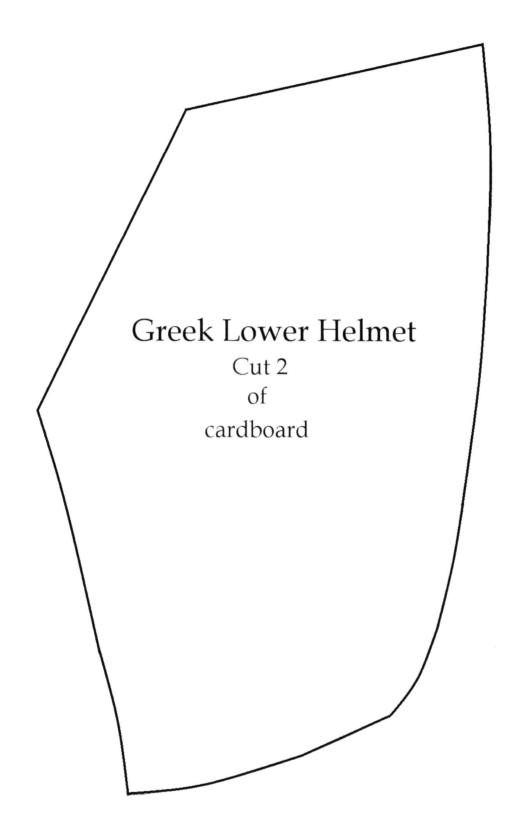

Greek Lower Helmet
Cut 2
of
cardboard

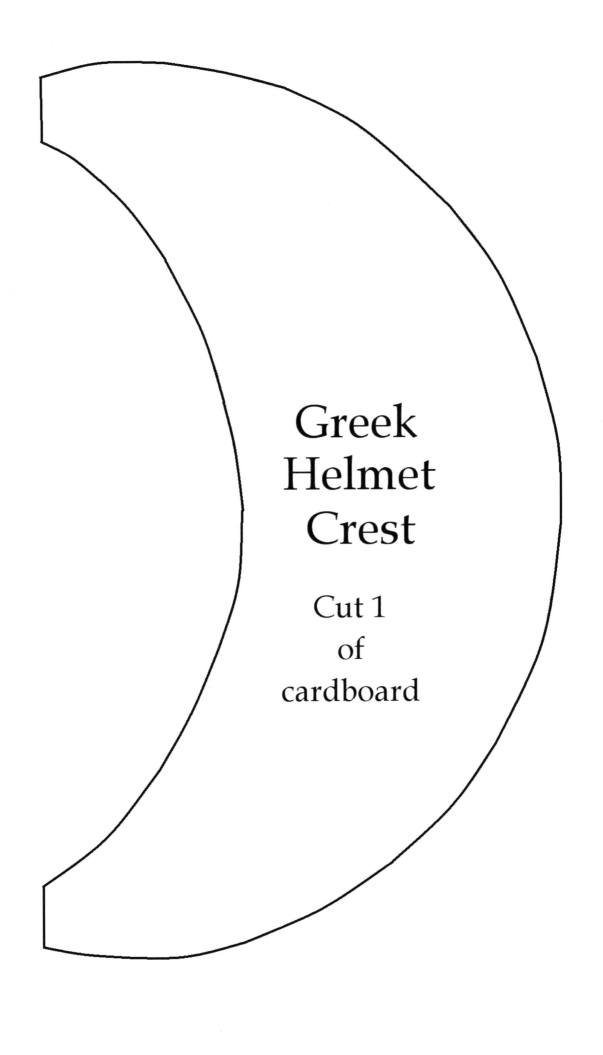

Greek
Helmet
Crest

Cut 1
of
cardboard

Cut 1
of
cardboard

Back of Helmet

CPSIA information can be obtained at www.ICGtesting.com
Printed in the USA
LVIW01n1726140115
422821LV00005B/43

9781942006053

5